Name ______________________ Class ______________ Date ______________

Skills Worksheet

Directed Reading

Lesson: Tobacco and Alcohol as Drugs

1. Why are alcohol and tobacco considered drugs?

____

AFFECTING THE MIND AND BODY

2. A plant with leaves that can be dried and mixed with chemicals to make products such as cigarettes and cigars is ______________________.

3. What effect does alcohol have on the body?

____

TOBACCO AND ALCOHOL ARE UNPREDICTABLE

4. List three factors that affect how a person will react to alcohol.

____

____

____

Lesson: Tobacco Products

CHEMICALS IN TOBACCO PRODUCTS

______ **5.** What is the name of the addictive drug found in tobacco products?

a. carbon monoxide
b. nicotine
c. tar
d. ETS

EARLY EFFECTS OF CIGARETTES

6. What is tar?

____

7. List three physical effects of smoking cigarettes.

____

____

____

ENVIRONMENTAL TOBACCO SMOKE

8. What is environmental tobacco smoke?

____

____

9. What health problems can be caused by ETS?

____

____

SMOKELESS TOBACCO

______**10.** Which of the following is a form of smokeless tobacco?

a. spit tobacco
b. snuff
c. chewing tobacco
d. All of the above

TOBACCO-RELATED DISEASE AND DEATH

11. Describe two serious diseases that smoking can cause.

____

____

Lesson: Alcohol

EARLY EFFECTS OF ALCOHOL

12. List three possible effects of consuming alcohol.

____

____

____

BLOOD ALCOHOL CONCENTRATION

13. Define intoxication.

____

____

14. The percentage of alcohol in a person's blood is called the

________________________.

LONG-TERM EFFECTS OF ALCOHOL

______**15.** Which of the following is a disease caused by consuming large amounts of alcohol?
a. emphysema
b. asthma
c. cirrhosis
d. None of the above

______**16.** Alcohol can increase the risk of
a. stroke.
b. high blood pressure.
c. heart disease.
d. All of the above

ALCOHOL AND PREGNANCY

17. A group of birth defects that can occur when an unborn baby is exposed to

alcohol is called ________________________.

DRUNK DRIVING

______**18.** Driving when even slightly intoxicated is dangerous because alcohol
a. slows down your ability to react.
b. impairs the ability to respond as quickly as usual.
c. impairs the ability to make responsible decisions.
d. All of the above

Lesson: Addiction

FORMING AN ADDICTION

19. The body's ability to resist the effects of a drug is called

________________________.

20. When a person needs a drug to feel normal, he or she has a(n)

____

ALCOHOLISM

21. Define *alcoholism.*

____

____

____

KICKING A HABIT

22. How can quitting an addiction to alcohol be dangerous?

____

____

____

____

Lesson: Feeling Pressure

PRESSURE FROM OTHER PEOPLE

23. Pressure from a friend or group of friends is called ____________________.

ADVERTISEMENTS

24. How do advertisements for tobacco and alcohol depict drug use?

____

____

____

____

GETTING THROUGH ROUGH TIMES

25. Can drugs solve problems? Explain your answer.

____

____

____

____

____

Lesson: Refusing Tobacco and Alcohol

WAYS TO REFUSE

26. Explain two ways you can refuse drugs.

PROVIDING ALTERNATIVES

27. List two alternatives to drinking alcohol you could suggest to a friend.

BUILD AN ACTIVE SOCIAL LIFE

28. Are drugs necessary for having fun? Explain your answer.

Name ______________________ Class ______________ Date ______________

Skills Worksheet

Concept Mapping

Lesson: Tobacco Products

Use the following terms to complete the concept map below: ***emphysema, cigarettes, tobacco products, cancer, nicotine, tar, addictive drug,*** **and** ***carbon monoxide.***

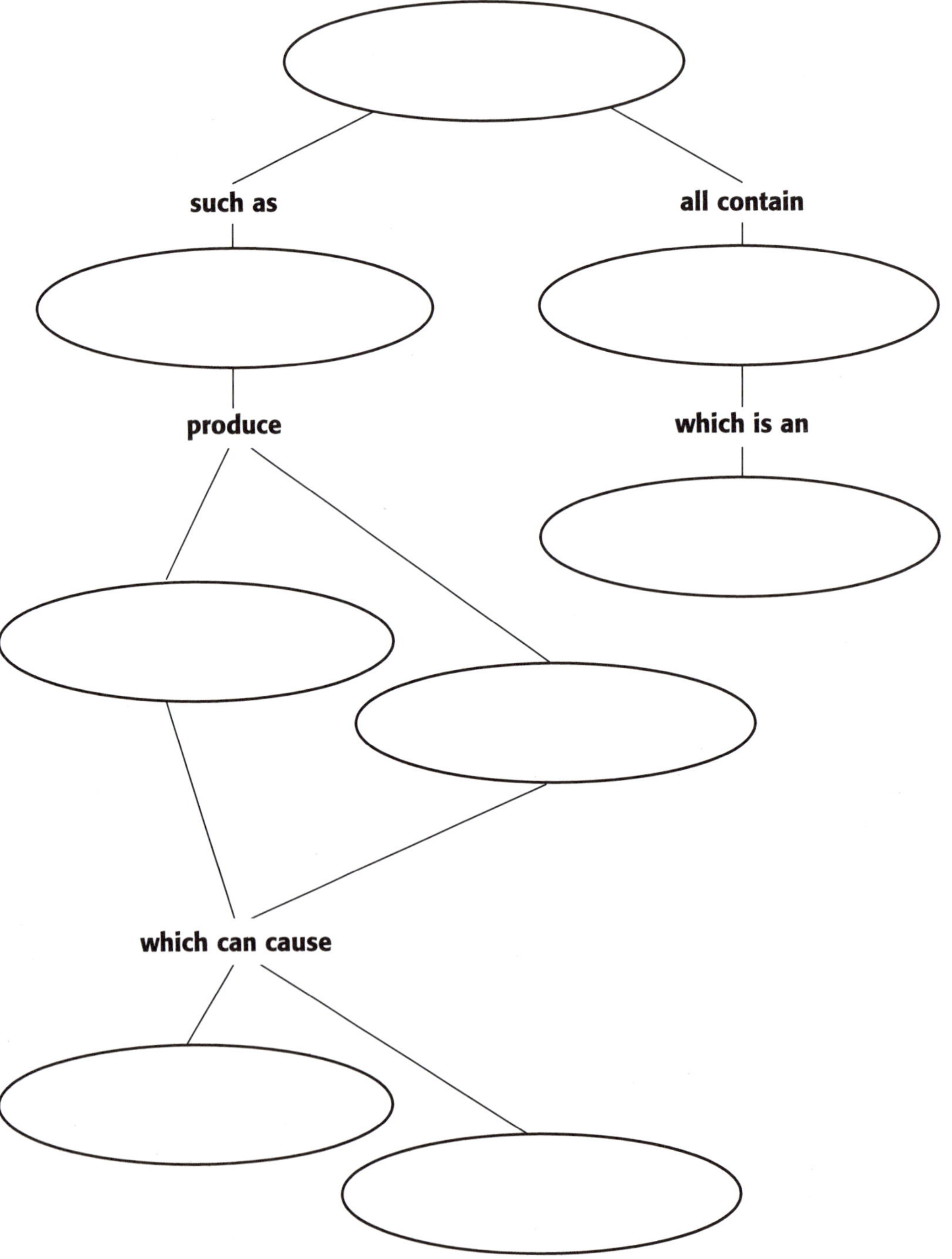

Name ______________________ Class ______________ Date ____________

Skills Worksheet

Concept Mapping

Lesson: Refusing Tobacco and Alcohol

Use the following terms to create a concept map below: *refusal skills, saying "no, thanks," giving a reason, friends, suggesting an alternative, advertisements, role models, pressure,* and *walking away.*

Name ______________________ Class ______________ Date ____________

Skills Worksheet

Concept Review

Lesson: Tobacco and Alcohol as Drugs

______ **1.** What factors can affect how a person will react to drinking alcohol?
- **a.** how much alcohol they have consumed in the past
- **b.** how much they weigh
- **c.** how much food is in their stomach
- **d.** All of the above

2. Explain why tobacco and alcohol are drugs.

____

____

____

3. Explain why people's reactions to tobacco and alcohol are unpredictable.

____

____

____

Lesson: Tobacco Products

4. What effect does carbon monoxide have on the body?

____

____

5. Explain the physical effects of tar.

____

____

____

6. List the early effects of smoking cigarettes.

____

____

____

Match each item in the right column to the correct term in the left column.

______ **7.** a dangerous chemical found in all tobacco products

______ **8.** a disease in which the lungs are so damaged that they cannot absorb enough oxygen

______ **9.** a mixture of exhaled smoke and smoke from the ends of cigarettes

______ **10.** a disease in which abnormal cells destroy healthy body tissues

______ **11.** a product made from chopped tobacco leaves that can be tucked under the lips

______ **12.** powdered tobacco that can be sniffed

a. ETS

b. nicotine

c. snuff

d. chewing tobacco

e. emphysema

f. cancer

Lesson: Alcohol

13. List three possible effects of intoxication.

____

____

____

14. The percentage of alcohol in a person's blood is called the

______________________.

15. Name two health problems caused by long-term alcohol abuse.

____

____

____

16. Explain how alcohol can impair your ability to drive.

____

____

17. What are two characteristics of babies born with fetal alcohol syndrome?

____

____

Lesson: Addiction

______**18.** The body's ability to resist the effects of a drug is called
- **a.** drug addiction.
- **b.** alcoholism.
- **c.** tolerance.
- **d.** None of the above

______**19.** Needing a drug in order to feel normal is called
- **a.** drug addiction.
- **b.** alcoholism.
- **c.** tolerance.
- **d.** None of the above

______**20.** A disease caused by addiction to alcohol is called
- **a.** drug addiction.
- **b.** alcoholism.
- **c.** tolerance.
- **d.** None of the above

21. Explain how alcoholism can affect the family of a person who has alcoholism.

____

____

____

22. Name three support programs for people who have alcoholism and for their families.

____

____

____

23. Explain why it is difficult to quit using drugs once a person is addicted.

____

____

____

____

____

Lesson: Feeling Pressure

24. Describe how each group of people can pressure teens to try tobacco and alcohol:

friends:

___

___

family:

___

___

role models:

___

___

25. Explain how peer pressure can be positive or negative.

___

___

26. How does the media pressure teens to use tobacco and alcohol?

___

___

___

Lesson: Refusing Tobacco and Alcohol

27. Describe two ways you can refuse tobacco or alcohol.

___

___

28. List three drug-free ways to be social.

___

___

___

Name ______________________ Class ______________ Date ____________

Skills Worksheet

Refusal Skills

Lesson: Feeling Pressure

Describe how you would use the refusal skills listed below to respond to the following scenario. Remember to be clear and choose your words carefully.

You are walking home from school with your friend Joanna. Joanna lights up a cigarette and offers you one. She tells you that everyone smokes and that smoking is cool.

1. **Say no.** How would you say no to Joanna?

____

____

2. **Offer an alternative.** What alternative could you offer Joanna?

____

____

3. **Stand your ground.** What would you do if Joanna kept pressuring you to smoke?

____

____

4. **Walk away.** Describe how you would get out of the situation.

____

____

5. **Plan ahead.** What could you do to avoid this situation? Who can help you practice refusing this action?

____

____

6. **Have a support system.** Who will stand by you when you make this decision? How can you use these people as support when refusing to do this action?

____

____

Name ______________________ Class ______________ Date ____________

Skills Worksheet

Refusal Skills

Lesson: Refusing Tobacco and Alcohol

Imagine that you are the advice columnist for the school paper. Answer the following letter from a fellow student.

Dear Know-It-All,

Last weekend I attended a party at a friend's house. I noticed that most of the other kids were drinking beer. My friend offered me a beer. He told me that everyone would think I was a baby if I did not drink it, and said that it would be safe to try beer with a big group of friends. Everyone around him agreed, so I drank the beer. It made me feel horrible! Please tell me what I should do if this happens again.

Sincerely,

Trying to Say No

Dear Trying:

Name ______________________ Class ______________ Date ____________

Skills Worksheet

Decision-Making Skills

Lesson: Tobacco Products

Read the following situation. Then, follow the steps below to decide what you would do in this situation.

Your two best friends, Bill and Dennis, have recently started smoking. The three of you have always walked home together every day after school. Now Bill and Dennis go to the park every day on the way home to smoke. You have been going with them. They always try to pressure you into smoking.

1. **Identify the problem.** What decision do you have to make?

____

____

2. **Consider your values.** What is important to you?

____

____

3. **List the options.** What possible actions could you take?

____

____

4. **Weigh the consequences.** List the pros and cons of each option.

____

____

5. **Decide and act.** Describe what you will do. Explain your decision.

____

____

6. **Evaluate your choice.** How do you feel about the action you took? Did you make a good decision? Would you take a different action if faced with the same scenario again?

____

____

Name ______________________________ Class ______________ Date ____________

Skills Worksheet

Decision-Making Skills

Lesson: Alcohol

Read the following story and then write an ending to the story in the space below.

Walter was at a party with some friends who had been drinking. His friend Nick's older sister, Carrie, drove him to the party. When it was time to leave, Walter noticed that Carrie was intoxicated. Walter knew that he should not get into the car if she was driving. However, he was worried about calling his parents for a ride home because they thought Walter was at the movies instead of a party.

What should Walter do? Be sure to answer this question in the ending to the story.

Name ______________________ Class ______________ Date ____________

Skills Worksheet

Cross-Disciplinary: Music

Lesson: Tobacco and Alcohol as Drugs

In a small group, write a jingle for a nonsmoking advertising campaign. Pick a familiar tune and then write new lyrics for the song. Write the lyrics below. Then perform your song for the class.

Sing to the tune of:

Name ______________________ Class ______________ Date ____________

Skills Worksheet

Cross-Disciplinary: Language Arts

Lesson: Alcohol

Write a short play about the effects of alcohol. Include at least three characters in your play. At least one character should be intoxicated. Show the effects of intoxication on this person and the people around him or her. Write your play on the lines below.

Name ______________________ Class ______________ Date ____________

Assessment

Quiz

Lesson: Tobacco and Alcohol as Drugs

Write the letter of the correct answer in the space provided.

______ **1.** Tobacco
  a. is a drug.
  b. can make people feel more alert.
  c. can make people feel more relaxed.
  d. All of the above

______ **2.** Which is NOT an effect of alcohol?
  a. It lowers heart rate.
  b. It speeds reaction time.
  c. It lowers breathing rate.
  d. It slows the mind.

______ **3.** Tobacco is used to make products such as
  a. cigars.
  b. smokeless tobacco.
  c. cigarettes.
  d. All of the above

______ **4.** Which factor affects how a person reacts to a drug?
  a. how much food is in their stomach
  b. their body weight
  c. how much they have used the drug in the past
  d. All of the above

______ **5.** Mixing alcohol or tobacco with another drug can
  a. change its effects.
  b. be good for you.
  c. help you solve your problems.
  d. None of the above

Name ______________________ Class ______________ Date ____________

Assessment

Quiz

Lesson: Tobacco Products

Write the letter of the correct answer in the space provided.

______ **1.** One dangerous chemical found in all tobacco products is
a. carbon monoxide.
b. tar.
c. ETS.
d. nicotine.

______ **2.** A dangerous gas in cigarette smoke is
a. carbon monoxide.
b. tar.
c. ETS.
d. nicotine.

______ **3.** A sticky substance that coats the lungs is
a. carbon monoxide.
b. tar.
c. ETS.
d. nicotine.

______ **4.** The mixture of exhaled smoke and smoke from the end of a cigarette is called
a. carbon monoxide.
b. tar.
c. ETS.
d. nicotine.

______ **5.** Some effects of cigarettes include
a. dulled taste buds.
b. yellow teeth.
c. difficulty breathing.
d. All of the above

______ **6.** Which is a harmless form of tobacco?
a. snuff
b. chewing tobacco
c. spit tobacco
d. None of the above

Name ______________________ Class ______________ Date ____________

Assessment

Quiz

Lesson: Alcohol

Match the definitions with the correct term. Write the letter in the space provided.

______ **1.** a group of birth defects that can occur when an unborn baby is exposed to alcohol

______ **2.** a disease that prevents the liver from working normally

______ **3.** a state of being affected by alcohol

______ **4.** the percentage of alcohol in the blood

a. intoxication
b. blood alcohol concentration
c. cirrhosis
d. fetal alcohol syndrome

Write the letter of the correct answer in the space provided.

______ **5.** How does alcohol affect a person's ability to drive?
a. It slows your reaction time.
b. It makes you see more clearly.
c. It makes you more alert.
d. It allows you to make responsible decisions.

______ **6.** Which is an effect of intoxication?
a. vomiting
b. passing out
c. tiredness
d. All of the above

Name ______________________ Class ______________ Date ____________

Assessment

Quiz

Lesson: Addiction

Write the letter of the correct answer in the space provided.

______ **1.** The body's ability to resist the effects of a drug is called
a. drug addiction.
b. tolerance.
c. alcoholism.
d. None of the above

______ **2.** Needing a drug to feel normal is called
a. drug addiction.
b. tolerance.
c. alcoholism.
d. None of the above

______ **3.** Which of the following is an effect of alcoholism?
a. difficulty making decisions
b. strange reactions to normal events
c. neglecting family and friends
d. All of the above

______ **4.** What can help people who have alcoholism and their families?
a. smoking
b. more alcohol
c. support programs
d. None of the above

______ **5.** Quitting an addiction to alcohol may require
a. hospitalization.
b. the person to give up.
c. small bits of alcohol to help the person get by.
d. All of the above

Name ________________________ Class ______________ Date ____________

Assessment

Quiz

Lesson: Feeling Pressure

Write the letter of the correct answer in the space provided.

______ **1.** Pressure to try tobacco or alcohol can come from
a. family members.
b. friends.
c. role models.
d. All of the above

______ **2.** Influence from a friend or group of friends is called
a. addiction.
b. peer pressure.
c. quitting.
d. None of the above

______ **3.** How can advertisements encourage people to use tobacco and drugs?
a. They make it look cool.
b. They do not show the negative side of drug use.
c. They make it look glamorous.
d. All of the above

______ **4.** Abusing tobacco and drugs will NOT
a. solve your problems.
b. cause you to become addicted.
c. negatively affect your health.
d. All of the above

______ **5.** You can solve problems by
a. drinking alcohol.
b. smoking cigarettes.
c. talking with others.
d. None of the above

Name ______________________________ Class ______________ Date ____________

Assessment

Quiz

Lesson: Refusing Tobacco and Alcohol

Write the letter of the correct answer in the space provided.

______ **1.** If you are not comfortable giving reasons for refusing drugs, you could just
- **a.** change the subject.
- **b.** walk away.
- **c.** offer an alternative.
- **d.** All of the above

______ **2.** A true friend will
- **a.** pressure you into using drugs.
- **b.** make fun of you if you refuse drugs.
- **c.** respect your decision to refuse drugs.
- **d.** All of the above

______ **3.** Which of the following is NOT a good excuse for refusing to do drugs?
- **a.** It's illegal.
- **b.** No thanks, I'm not interested.
- **c.** No thanks, I want to be ready for the game tomorrow.
- **d.** Maybe I'll try it later, after school.

______ **4.** Which of the following is an example of a drug-free social activity?
- **a.** sports team
- **b.** volunteer program
- **c.** music group
- **d.** All of the above

______ **5.** Illegal drugs are
- **a.** the only way to have fun.
- **b.** dangerous and unpredictable.
- **c.** good for you.
- **d.** All of the above

Assessment

Chapter Test

Tobacco and Alcohol

USING VOCABULARY

Use the terms from the following list to complete the sentences below. Each term may be used only once. Some terms will not be used.

tobacco	alcohol	nicotine
ETS	intoxication	cirrhosis
alcoholism	peer pressure	
cancer	blood alcohol concentration	

1. The state of being affected by alcohol is called ______________________.

2. A liquid that can affect the way people think and act is

______________________.

3. The disease caused by addiction to alcohol is called

______________________.

4. A long-term effect of using tobacco products is ______________________.

5. Encouragement from a friend to smoke a cigarette or drink alcohol is called

______________________.

6. The percentage of alcohol in a person's blood is called the

______________________.

UNDERSTANDING CONCEPTS

Write the letter of the correct answer in the space provided.

______ **7.** A disease in which the liver is damaged and does not work normally is called

a. cancer.
b. FAS.
c. cirrhosis.
d. emphysema.

______ **8.** Another name for ETS is

a. tobacco.
b. secondhand smoke.
c. nicotine.
d. tar.

______ **9.** A disease that affects the unborn babies of women who drink alcohol during pregnancy is called
a. cancer.
b. FAS.
c. cirrhosis.
d. emphysema.

______ **10.** A disease in which the lungs get so damaged that they cannot absorb enough oxygen is called
a. cancer.
b. FAS.
c. cirrhosis.
d. emphysema.

______ **11.** A plant with leaves that can be dried and mixed with chemicals to make cigarettes and other products is called
a. tobacco.
b. nicotine.
c. alcohol.
d. tar.

______ **12.** The addictive drug found in cigarettes is called
a. tobacco.
b. nicotine.
c. alcohol.
d. tar.

______ **13.** The percentage of alcohol in a person's blood is called
a. blood intoxication.
b. cirrhosis.
c. intoxication.
d. blood alcohol concentration.

______ **14.** Which is NOT an early effect of cigarette smoking?
a. emphysema
b. bad breath
c. smelly clothes and hair
d. dulled taste buds

15. Explain the factors that affect how people will react to a drug.

____

____

____

16. Explain how carbon monoxide and tar damage the body.

____

____

____

17. What factors affect blood alcohol concentration?

____

____

____

____

____

18. Explain how advertisements can be a source of pressure to use tobacco and alcohol.

____

____

____

____

____

____

CRITICAL THINKING

19. Explain how tolerance is related to drug addiction.

____

____

____

____

____

____

____

20. Serena is spending the night at her friend Emily's house. After Emily's parents go to bed, Emily opens up the refrigerator and pours a glass of wine for herself and Serena. Describe and explain three ways that Serena could refuse the alcohol.

INTERPRETING GRAPHICS

Examine the diagram below, and answer the questions that follow.

21. About what percentage of smokers want to quit?

22. About what percentage succeed in permanently quitting smoking?

23. How does looking at this graph influence your decision to start smoking or not?

Assessment

Performance-Based Assessment

Refusing Tobacco and Alcohol

INTRODUCTION

You've read about ways to refuse tobacco and alcohol. Now you will have a chance to practice refusing when you are offered tobacco or alcohol.

OBJECTIVE

- Keep in mind that your teacher will be observing and grading your in-class behavior as well as your written responses. In particular, your teacher will be noting your ability to follow the given procedures, how well you follow classroom safety guidelines, and your methods and reasoning in solving problems.
- Try not to let what others are doing influence your work. Remember that a problem often has several acceptable solutions.
- Do not talk to other students unless you are working in a group. Talk only to members of your group and try not to disturb other students.
- Use only the materials provided.

MATERIALS AND EQUIPMENT

- pencils
- notepads

PROCEDURE

1. Select a partner.
2. Write two skits that deal with refusing alcohol and tobacco. One person should write a skit in which a person is offered alcohol or tobacco and does not refuse. The skit should explore the consequences of not refusing the drug. The other person should write a different skit in which a person is offered alcohol or tobacco and does refuse. That skit should demonstrate what technique the person uses to refuse.
3. Practice performing the skits with your partner.
4. Perform your skits for the entire class.
5. Pay careful attention as other pairs of students perform their skits.

ANALYSIS

Answer the following questions in the space provided. Support your answers by explaining your reasoning.

6. What are the consequences of not refusing?

____

____

____

7. How could the person in the first skit have refused the tobacco or alcohol?

____

____

____

8. What technique did the person in the second skit use to refuse the tobacco or alcohol?

____

____

____

9. Did the consequences or refusal strategies in the skits of other students surprise you, or were any skits especially effective? Explain your answer.

____

____

____

____

Name ______________________________ Class ______________ Date ____________

Activity

Datasheet for In-Text Activity

Understanding Blood Alcohol Concentration (BAC)

Set up two medium glasses, one small glass, and one large glass. Fill each with water colored by red food coloring. Add one drop of blue food coloring to a medium glass and three drops to each of the other glasses. Observe and record the color changes in the table below.

Glass	Drops of Food Coloring	Observations: color change
med. glass #1	1	
med. glass #2	3	
small glass	3	
large glass	3	

ANALYSIS

1. If the blue food coloring were alcohol and the red water were blood, which glass would have the highest BAC? Which would have the lowest?

____

____

____

____

____

____

2. How does the size of the glass affect the BAC?

____

____

____

____

____

____

____

Name ______________________ Class ______________ Date ____________

Activity

Life Skills: Communicating Effectively

Lesson: Addiction

COMMUNICATING WITH FRIENDS

Read the following situation. Then answer the questions.

Your friend Nora has been drinking a lot of alcohol for the past few months. You used to do things with her on the weekends, but now all she does is go to parties where alcohol is served. You went with her once and felt very uncomfortable because she was intoxicated and acting totally out of control. Nora sneaks some of her parents' alcohol every day and brings it to school. She goes to her locker several times a day to sneak a drink. You've asked Nora why she's doing this, and she told you it makes her feel good—she even said she drinks by herself when she's home alone. She can't even go one day without having a drink now.

1. Does Nora have a problem with alcohol? Explain your answer.

____

____

____

2. How could you communicate your concerns to Nora?

____

____

____

3. Where could you suggest Nora go for support and to get help with her problem?

____

____

____

4. If Nora will not get help on her own, to whom will you go with your concerns?

____

____

____

____

Name ______________________ Class ______________ Date ______________

Activity

Life Skills: Evaluating Media Messages

Lesson: Feeling Pressure

ADVERTISING ALCOHOL AND TOBACCO

Find several magazines that contain advertisements for alcohol and tobacco products.

1. Which magazines did you find?

2. Who typically reads each magazine?

3. Describe some of the ads for alcohol. How do the ads portray people who drink alcohol?

4. Describe some of the ads for tobacco products. How do the ads portray people who use tobacco products?

5. Explain how these images compare to the real effects of using alcohol and tobacco products.

Name ______________________ Class ______________ Date ____________

Activity

Enrichment Activity

Lesson: Tobacco and Alcohol as Drugs

Survey 30 students at your school. Ask each student the following questions:

- Is tobacco a drug?
- Is alcohol a drug?

Tally the results of your survey. Now make two circle graphs using a computer graphing program if possible. One graph should show the percentage of students who think tobacco is a drug compared with the percentage of those who do not. The other graph should show the percentage of students who think alcohol is a drug compared with the percentage of those who do not. Was there anything surprising about the results of your survey? Write a short paragraph to explain.

Lesson: Tobacco Products

Find an adult who has smoked cigarettes for many years. Interview this adult about the effects of smoking. You may want to ask the following questions.

- How old were you when you started smoking?
- How many years have you been a smoker?
- Why did you start smoking?
- Have you ever tried to quit smoking? How many times? What methods did you try to help you quit smoking?
- Are you experiencing any health problems from smoking?
- If you were a teen today, would you start smoking?

Then, write three paragraphs that summarize the interview.

Lesson: Alcohol

Use the Internet to research the laws regarding driving while intoxicated in your state. Find out what the highest legal blood alcohol concentration is for driving a car. Research what happens if you get caught driving while intoxicated and what punishments you could face. Record your sources on the lines below. Then, prepare a one-page research report that presents your findings.

____

____

____

____

Lesson: Addiction

Go to the library and do research on alcoholism. Find out the causes and effects of alcoholism. Locate statistics that tell approximately how many people in the United States suffer from alcoholism. Research the various support programs for people with alcoholism. Find out how hospitals and rehabilitation centers help people recover from alcoholism. Prepare an oral presentation that summarizes your research. If possible, use a computer graphing program to help create any charts or graphs you might use.

Lesson: Feeling Pressure

Find articles, advertisements, and photographs that glamorize the use of alcohol and tobacco. Cut these out and paste them onto a large piece of poster board to make a collage. Your collage should show how using these drugs is glamorized by the media. Then, write down the damaging effects of tobacco and alcohol on a piece of paper. Cut the paper into strips, with one negative effect on each strip. Paste these negative effects over the items that glamorize the use of alcohol and tobacco products.

Lesson: Refusing Tobacco and Alcohol

Write a script for a video that demonstrates how to refuse alcohol and tobacco products. Assume the video will be used to teach younger children to say no to alcohol and tobacco products. Make sure your video covers the following topics:

- different ways to say no
- providing alternatives
- social activities that do not involve alcohol and tobacco products

Name ______________________ Class ______________ Date ____________

Activity

Health Inventory

Resisting Peer Pressure

Read each of the following statements about peer pressure. Then, put a checkmark next to each statement that describes your behavior.

______________________ **1.** If a friend were smoking a cigarette and offered me one, I would accept and smoke the cigarette.

______________________ **2.** If I were with a group of other people who were smoking, I would smoke too, just to fit in.

______________________ **3.** If a friend were drinking a beer and offered me one, I would accept and drink it.

______________________ **4.** If I were at a social gathering where most people were drinking alcohol, I would drink too.

______________________ **5.** When I see celebrities smoking, I want to smoke, too.

______________________ **6.** When I see celebrities drinking alcohol, I want to drink alcohol, too.

______________________ **7.** If someone who had been drinking offered me a ride home, I would accept so that I wouldn't offend him or her.

______________________ **8.** I have difficulty resisting peer pressure when faced with difficult decisions.

Give yourself one point for each checkmark. Write your score here ______.

0: You are good at resisting peer pressure.

1–2: You may be able to resist peer pressure sometimes, but you could work to resist it more consistently.

3–4: You should practice strategies for resisting peer pressure.

More than 4: You know few strategies for resisting peer pressure. You may want to talk to a trusted adult about how to make better decisions for yourself.

Name ______________________ Class ______________ Date ____________

Activity

Health Behavior Contract

Tobacco and Alcohol

My Goals: I, ______________________________, will accomplish one or more of the following goals:

I will not use tobacco or alcohol.

I will find out where to go for help if a friend suffers from alcoholism.

I will use refusal skills if alcohol and tobacco are offered to me.

Other: ____

____

My Reasons: By abstaining from tobacco and alcohol and using refusal skills if someone offers tobacco or alcohol to me, I will protect my health. By knowing how to deal with alcoholism, I will be prepared to help my friends and family.

Other: ____

____

My Values: Personal values that will help me meet my goals are

____

____

____

My Plan: The actions I will take to meet my goals are

____

____

____

Evaluation: I will use my Health Journal to keep a log of actions I took to fulfill this contract. After 1 month, I will evaluate my goals. I will adjust my plan if my goals are not being met. If my goals are being met, I will consider setting additional goals.

Signed ______________________

Date ______________________

Name ______________________ Class ______________ Date ____________

Activity

At-Home Activity

Tobacco and Alcohol

Scan magazines and newspapers to see an advertisement that encourages alcohol or tobacco use. Discuss the advertisement with a parent or caregiver.

1. Describe the advertisement.

____

____

____

2. What reasons does the advertisement give for using alcohol or tobacco?

____

____

____

3. What age group do you think the advertisement is trying to reach?

____

____

____

4. Do you think the advertisement is convincing? Explain.

____

____

____

Attach the advertisement to the back of this sheet.

The signatures below verify that our discussion has taken place.

______________________________________ ______________

Student Signature Class Period

______________________________________ ______________

Parent or Guardian Signature Date

Name ______________________ Class ____________ Date ____________

Activity

Actividad En Casa

El tabaco y el alcohol

Por revistas y periódicos, busque un anuncio comercial que estimule el uso del alcohol o del tabaco. Discuta el anuncio con su padre/madre/tutor y escriba las respuestas aquí.

1. Describa el anuncio.

____

____

____

2. ¿Qué razones da el anuncio por usar o el alcohol o el tabaco?

____

____

____

3. A su parecer, ¿a qué edad de personas se dirige el anuncio?

____

____

____

4. ¿Lo/La convence el anuncio a Ud.? Explique.

____

____

____

Las firmas verifican que discutimos esta actividad juntos.

______________________________ ______________________

Firma de Estudiante | Período de Clase(la Salud)

______________________________ ______________________

Firma de Padre/Madre/Tutor | Fecha

Lesson Plan

Lesson: Tobacco and Alcohol as Drugs

Pacing

45 minutes

Objectives

1. Explain why tobacco and alcohol are drugs.

Standards Covered

1.1 Explain the relationship between positive health behaviors and the prevention of injury, illness, disease, and premature death.

1.6 Describe ways to reduce risks related to adolescent health problems.

6.3 Predict how decisions regarding health behaviors have consequences for self and others.

KEY
SE = Student Edition   **ATE** = Annotated Teacher Edition
CRF = Chapter Resource File

CHAPTER OPENER

❑ **Health IQ, SE** To assess student knowledge about tobacco and alcohol, have students answer the Health IQ questions. Answers are at the bottom of the test.

FOCUS

❑ **Bellringer, ATE** Students list alcohol- and tobacco-related health risks.

❑ **Bellringer Transparency** Use this transparency as students enter the classroom and find their seats.

❑ **Start Off Write, SE** Ask students to write an answer to the following question: "What is dangerous about tobacco and alcohol?"

MOTIVATE

❑ **Activity, Poster Project, ATE** Students make a poster that discourages people from using tobacco and alcohol. **[GENERAL]**

TEACH

- ❑ **Group Activity, Skit, ATE** This activity asks students to write a skit about mixing alcohol and medicine. **[General]**
- ❑ **Reteaching, Different Reactions, ATE** This activity reinforces the different effects that alcohol can have on different people. **[Basic]**
- ❑ **Cross-Disciplinary: Music, CRF** This worksheet asks students to write a jingle for a nonsmoking ad campaign. **[General]**

CLOSE

- ❑ **Lesson Quiz, ATE** Students answer 2 questions about tobacco and alcohol. **[General]**
- ❑ **Lesson Quiz, CRF** Students answer 5 questions about tobacco and alcohol. **[General]**
- ❑ **Concept Review, CRF** This exercise reinforces the material covered in the lesson. **[General]**

HOMEWORK

- ❑ **Lesson Review, SE** Assign questions 1–6 for review, homework, or quiz.

OTHER RESOURCE OPTIONS

- ❑ **go.hrw.com** For worksheets, videos, and other teaching aids related to this chapter, visit the HRW Web site and type in the keyword HD4TOA.
- ❑ **VideoSelect** Videos related to the chapter topics may be found at go.hrw.com. Type in the keyword HD4TOAV.
- ❑ **Guided Audio CD Program** Tobacco and Alcohol. The audio program is a reading of the chapter content for ELL students, auditory learners, and struggling readers.
- ❑ **Enrichment Activity, CRF** Students conduct a survey about alcohol and tobacco. **[Advanced]**
- ❑ **Directed Reading, CRF** The worksheet guides struggling readers or ELL students through the lesson content. **[Basic]**

Lesson Plan

Lesson: Tobacco Products

Pacing

45 minutes

Objectives

1. Describe early effects of smoking.
2. Discuss health problems caused by smokeless tobacco.
3. Describe two diseases caused by long-term use of tobacco products.

Standards Covered

1.1 Explain the relationship between positive health behaviors and the prevention of injury, illness, disease, and premature death.

1.5 Analyze how environment and personal health are interrelated.

1.8 Describe how lifestyles, pathogens, family history, and other risk factors are related to the cause or prevention of disease and other health problems.

6.3 Predict how decisions regarding health behaviors have consequences for self and others.

KEY
SE = Student Edition **ATE** = Annotated Teacher Edition
CRF = Chapter Resource File

FOCUS

- ❑ **Bellringer, ATE** Students draw a picture showing the effects of smoking cigarettes.
- ❑ **Bellringer Transparency** Use this transparency as students enter the classroom and find their seats.
- ❑ **Start Off Write, SE** Ask students to write an answer to the following question: "How can tobacco smoke harm a nonsmoker?"

MOTIVATE

- ❑ **Discussion, Why Do Smokers Smoke? ATE** Students discuss the reasons that people smoke. **[GENERAL]**

TEACH

- ❑ **Life Skills Activity, Communicating Effectively, SE** This activity asks students to write a story about the effects of using tobacco products. **[GENERAL]**
- ❑ **Activity, Research, ATE** This activity asks students to research more about smoking and its health hazards. **[ADVANCED]**

Lesson Plan *continued*

- ❑ **Group Activity, Poster Project, ATE** This activity asks students to make posters illustrating the harmful effects of environmental tobacco smoke. **[GENERAL]**
- ❑ **Decision-Making Skills, CRF** This worksheet helps students practice making decisions about smoking. **[GENERAL]**

CLOSE

- ❑ **Lesson Quiz, ATE** Students answer 3 questions about tobacco products. **[GENERAL]**
- ❑ **Lesson Quiz, CRF** Students answer 6 questions about tobacco products. **[GENERAL]**
- ❑ **Concept Review, CRF** This exercise reinforces the material covered in the lesson. **[GENERAL]**

HOMEWORK

- ❑ **Lesson Review, SE** Assign questions 1–5 for review, homework, or quiz.
- ❑ **Concept Mapping, CRF** Students identify and map terms related to tobacco. **[GENERAL]**

OTHER RESOURCE OPTIONS

- ❑ **Internet Connect** Tobacco, HealthLinks Code HD4101. Students research Internet sources about tobacco products.
- ❑ **go.hrw.com** For worksheets, videos, and other teaching aids related to this chapter, visit the HRW Web site and type in the keyword HD4TOA.
- ❑ **VideoSelect** Videos related to the chapter topics may be found at go.hrw.com. Type in the keyword HD4TOAV.
- ❑ **Guided Audio CD Program** Tobacco and Alcohol. The audio program is a reading of the chapter content for ELL students, auditory learners, and struggling readers.
- ❑ **Enrichment Activity, CRF** Students interview an adult who smokes. **[ADVANCED]**
- ❑ **Directed Reading CRF** The worksheet guides struggling readers or ELL students through the lesson content. **[BASIC]**

Lesson Plan

Lesson: Alcohol

Pacing

25 minutes

Objectives

1. Discuss the effects of intoxication.
2. Name two health problems caused by long-term alcohol abuse.
3. Describe how alcohol impairs the ability to drive.

Standards Covered

1.1 Explain the relationship between positive health behaviors and the prevention of injury, illness, disease, and premature death.

1.6 Describe ways to reduce risks related to adolescent health problems.

1.8 Describe how lifestyles, pathogens, family history, and other risk factors are related to the cause or prevention of disease and other health problems.

6.3 Predict how decisions regarding health behaviors have consequences for self and others.

KEY
SE = Student Edition **ATE** = Annotated Teacher Edition
CRF = Chapter Resource File

FOCUS

- ❑ **Bellringer, ATE** This activity tests students' knowledge of alcohol content.
- ❑ **Bellringer Transparency** Use this transparency as students enter the classroom and find their seats.
- ❑ **Start Off Write, SE** Ask students to write an answer to the following question: "How does alcohol affect a person's behavior?"

MOTIVATE

- ❑ **Discussion, Anti-alcohol Messages, ATE** Students are asked their opinions on anti-alcohol messages. **[General]**

TEACH

- ❑ **Teaching Transparency** Alcohol Content. Use this graphic to help students understand the amounts of alcohol in different drinks.
- ❑ **Teaching Transparency** Fatal Auto Accidents Caused by Drunk Drivers. Use this graphic to help students understand how alcohol impairs the ability to drive.

Lesson Plan *continued*

- ❑ **Hands-On Activity, Understanding Blood Alcohol Concentration, SE** This activity asks students to investigate blood alcohol content.
- ❑ **Datasheet for In-Text Activity, Understanding Blood Alcohol Concentration, CRF** Students use this worksheet to record data for the Hands-On Activity.
- ❑ **Activity, Skit, ATE** This activity asks students to research the consequences of underage drinking. **[GENERAL]**
- ❑ **Inclusion Strategies, ATE** This activity helps students understand the dangers of driving while intoxicated. **[BASIC]**

CLOSE

- ❑ **Lesson Quiz, ATE** Students answer 3 questions about alcohol. **[GENERAL]**
- ❑ **Lesson Quiz, CRF** Students answer 6 questions about alcohol. **[GENERAL]**
- ❑ **Concept Review, CRF** This exercise reinforces the material covered in the lesson. **[GENERAL]**

HOMEWORK

- ❑ **Lesson Review, SE** Assign questions 1–4 for review, homework, or quiz.
- ❑ **Decision-Making Skills, CRF** students must decide whether or not to accept a ride with someone who has been drinking. **[GENERAL]**
- ❑ **Cross-Disciplinary: Language Arts, CRF** Students write a play about the effects of alcohol. **[GENERAL]**

OTHER RESOURCE OPTIONS

- ❑ **Internet Connect** Blood Alcohol Concentration, HealthLinks Code HD4016; Drunk Driving, HealthLinks Code HD4032. Students research Internet sources about blood alcohol concentration and drunk driving.
- ❑ **go.hrw.com** For worksheets, videos, and other teaching aids related to this chapter, visit the HRW Web site and type in the keyword HD4TOA.
- ❑ **VideoSelect** Videos related to the chapter topics may be found at go.hrw.com. Type in the keyword HD4TOA.
- ❑ **Guided Audio CD Program** Tobacco and Alcohol. The audio program is a reading of the chapter content for ELL students, auditory learners, and struggling readers.
- ❑ **Enrichment Activity, CRF** Students research their state laws regarding driving while intoxicated. **[ADVANCED]**
- ❑ **Directed Reading, CRF** The worksheet guides struggling readers or ELL students through the lesson content. **[BASIC]**

Lesson Plan

Lesson: Addiction

Pacing

20 minutes

Objectives

1. Explain how alcoholism affects the alcohol user and his or her family.
2. Describe how difficult it is to quit using drugs once a person is addicted.

Standards Covered

1.1 Explain the relationship between positive health behaviors and the prevention of injury, illness, disease, and premature death.

2.1 Analyze the validity of health information, products, and services.

2.6 Describe situations requiring professional health services.

6.3 Predict how decisions regarding health behaviors have consequences for self and others.

KEY
SE = Student Edition **ATE** = Annotated Teacher Edition
CRF = Chapter Resource File

FOCUS

❑ **Bellringer, ATE** Students write a paragraph about the difficulty of breaking a strong habit.

❑ **Bellringer Transparency** Use this transparency as students enter the classroom and find their seats.

❑ **Start Off Write, SE** Ask students to write an answer to the following question: "Where can people find help for an addiction to alcohol?"

MOTIVATE

❑ **Discussion, A Widespread Problem, ATE** Students discuss the problem of alcoholism in society. **[General]**

TEACH

❑ **Activity, How to Quit, ATE** This activity asks students to research products that help people quit drinking alcohol or using tobacco. **[Advanced]**

❑ **Inclusion Strategies, ATE** This activity helps students understand addiction. **[General]**

❑ **Life Skills: Communicating Effectively, CRF** Students discuss how they would help a friend with an alcohol addiction. **[General]**

Lesson Plan *continued*

CLOSE

- ❑ **Lesson Quiz, ATE** Students answer 3 questions about addiction. **[General]**
- ❑ **Lesson Quiz, CRF** Students answer 5 questions about addiction. **[General]**
- ❑ **Concept Review, CRF** This exercise reinforces the material covered in the lesson. **[General]**

HOMEWORK

- ❑ **Lesson Review, SE** Assign questions 1–3 for review, homework, or quiz.

OTHER RESOURCE OPTIONS

- ❑ **Internet Connect** Drug and Alcohol Abuse, HealthLinks Code HD4029; Alcoholism, HealthLinks Code HD4007. Students research Internet sources about drug and alcohol abuse and alcoholism.
- ❑ **go.hrw.com** For worksheets, videos, and other teaching aids related to this chapter, visit the HRW Web site and type in the keyword HD4TOA.
- ❑ **VideoSelect** Videos related to the chapter topics may be found at go.hrw.com. Type in the keyword HD4TOAV.
- ❑ **Guided Audio CD Program** Tobacco and Alcohol. The audio program is a reading of the chapter content for ELL students, auditory learners, and struggling readers.
- ❑ **Enrichment Activity, CRF** Students research alcoholism. **[Advanced]**
- ❑ **Directed Reading, CRF** The worksheet guides struggling readers or ELL students through the lesson content. **[Basic]**

Lesson Plan

Lesson: Feeling Pressure

Pacing

20 minutes

Objectives

1. Describe how friends, family, and role models pressure teens to try tobacco and alcohol.
2. Explain how peer pressure can be positive or negative.
3. Discuss how the media can influence teens about drugs.

Standards Covered

1.1 Explain the relationship between positive health behaviors and the prevention of injury, illness, disease, and premature death.

1.4 Describe how family and peers influence the health of adolescents.

2.1 Analyze the validity of health information, products, and services.

2.3 Analyze how media influences the selection of health information and products.

4.2 Analyze how messages from media and other sources influence health behaviors.

4.4 Analyze how information from peers influences health.

5.3 Demonstrate healthy ways to express needs, wants, and feelings.

5.6 Demonstrate refusal and negotiation skills to enhance health.

6.2 Analyze how health-related decisions are influenced by individuals, family, and community values.

KEY
SE = Student Edition   **ATE** = Annotated Teacher Edition
CRF = Chapter Resource File

FOCUS

- ❑ **Bellringer, ATE** Students describe a time when they experienced peer pressure.
- ❑ **Bellringer Transparency** Use this transparency as students enter the classroom and find their seats.
- ❑ **Start Off Write, SE** Ask students to write an answer to the following question: "Why might a person try alcohol or tobacco?"

MOTIVATE

- ❑ **Activity, Poster Project, ATE** Students make a poster to illustrate peer pressure. **[GENERAL]**

TEACH

- ❑ **Group Activity, Advertising, ATE** This activity asks students to create advertisements about the true effects of alcohol. **[GENERAL]**
- ❑ **Life Skill Builder, Evaluating Media Messages, ATE** This activity asks students to analyze tobacco advertisements. **[GENERAL]**
- ❑ **Refusal Skills, CRF** Students practice refusing a cigarette. **[GENERAL]**
- ❑ **Life Skills: Evaluating Media Messages, CRF** Students analyze alcohol and tobacco advertisements. **[GENERAL]**

CLOSE

- ❑ **Lesson Quiz, ATE** Students answer 2 questions about feeling pressure. **[GENERAL]**
- ❑ **Lesson Quiz, CRF** Students answer 5 questions about feeling pressure. **[GENERAL]**
- ❑ **Concept Review, CRF** This exercise reinforces the material covered in the lesson. **[GENERAL]**

HOMEWORK

- ❑ **Lesson Review, SE** Assign questions 1–4 for review, homework, or quiz.

OTHER RESOURCE OPTIONS

- ❑ **go.hrw.com** For worksheets, videos, and other teaching aids related to this chapter, visit the HRW Web site and type in the keyword HD4TOA.
- ❑ **VideoSelect** Videos related to the chapter topics may be found at go.hrw.com. Type in the keyword HD4TOAV.
- ❑ **Guided Audio CD Program** Tobacco and Alcohol. The audio program is a reading of the chapter content for ELL students, auditory learners, and struggling readers.
- ❑ **Enrichment Activity, CRF** Students create a collage that shows how the media glamorizes alcohol and tobacco. **[ADVANCED]**
- ❑ **Directed Reading, CRF** The worksheet guides struggling readers or ELL students through the lesson content. **[BASIC]**

Lesson Plan

Lesson: Refusing Tobacco and Alcohol

Pacing

20 minutes

Objectives

1. Discuss ways to refuse tobacco or alcohol.
2. Describe drug-free ways to be social.

Standards Covered

1.1 Explain the relationship between positive health behaviors and the prevention of injury, illness, disease, and premature death.

1.6 Describe ways to reduce risks related to adolescent health problems.

3.4 Demonstrate strategies to improve or maintain personal and family health.

3.6 Demonstrate ways to avoid and reduce threatening situations.

4.4 Analyze how information from peers influences health.

5.6 Demonstrate refusal and negotiation skills to enhance health.

6.3 Predict how decisions regarding health behaviors have consequences for self and others.

KEY
SE = Student Edition **ATE** = Annotated Teacher Edition
CRF = Chapter Resource File

FOCUS

- ❑ **Bellringer, ATE** Students make a list of drug-free ways to have fun.
- ❑ **Bellringer Transparency** Use this transparency as students enter the classroom and find their seats.
- ❑ **Start Off Write, SE** Ask students to write an answer to the following question: "What can you do to resist an offer of tobacco or alcohol?"

MOTIVATE

- ❑ **Activity, Role-Play, ATE** Students demonstrate how to resist an offer to smoke cigarettes. **[GENERAL]**

Lesson Plan *continued*

TEACH

- ❑ **Life Skills Activity, Using Refusal Skills, SE** Students write a skit about refusing drugs. [GENERAL]
- ❑ **Demonstration, Environmental Tobacco Smoke, ATE** This activity demonstrates the effects of environmental tobacco smoke. [BASIC]
- ❑ **Refusal Skills, CRF** Students practice refusing alcohol. [GENERAL]
- ❑ **Concept Mapping, CRF** Students map terms related to refusing tobacco and alcohol. [GENERAL]

CLOSE

- ❑ **Lesson Quiz, ATE** Students answer 3 questions about refusing tobacco and alcohol. [GENERAL]
- ❑ **Lesson Quiz, CRF** Students answer 5 questions about refusing tobacco and alcohol. [GENERAL]
- ❑ **Concept Review, CRF** This exercise reinforces the material covered in the lesson. [GENERAL]

HOMEWORK

- ❑ **Lesson Review, SE** Assign questions 1–4 for review, homework, or quiz.

OTHER RESOURCE OPTIONS

- ❑ **go.hrw.com** For worksheets, videos, and other teaching aids related to this chapter, visit the HRW Web site and type in the keyword HD4TOA.
- ❑ **VideoSelect** Videos related to the chapter topics may be found at go.hrw.com. Type in the keyword HD4TOAV.
- ❑ **Guided Audio CD Program** Tobacco and Alcohol. The audio program is a reading of the chapter content for ELL students, auditory learners, and struggling readers.
- ❑ **Enrichment Activity, CRF** Students write a script for a video that demonstrates how to refuse alcohol and tobacco products. [ADVANCED]
- ❑ **Directed Reading, CRF** The worksheet guides struggling readers or ELL students through the lesson content. [BASIC]

Lesson Plan

End of Chapter Review and Assessment

Pacing

90 minutes

KEY
SE = Student Edition **ATE** = Annotated Teacher Edition
CRF = Chapter Resource File

REVIEW

- ❑ **Chapter Review, SE** Assign questions to review the material for this chapter. Use the assignment guide to customize review for lessons covered.
- ❑ **Concept Review, CRF** Vocabulary and concept review for each lesson. **[General]**

ASSESSMENT

- ❑ **Chapter Test, Tobacco and Alcohol, CRF** Assign questions for general level chapter assessment. **[General]**

ALTERNATIVE ASSESSMENT

- ❑ **Alternative Assessment, Tobacco Pamphlets, ATE** Assign this activity for general level assessment for the lesson *Tobacco Products.* **[General]**
- ❑ **Alternative Assessment, Alcohol Essay, ATE** Assign this activity for advanced level assessment for the lesson *Alcohol.* **[Advanced]**
- ❑ **Performance-Based Assessment, Refusing Tobacco and Alcohol, CRF** Students write and perform two skits dealing with refusing tobacco and alcohol. **[General]**
- ❑ **Test Generator** One-Stop Planner. Create a customized homework, quiz, or test using the HRE Test Generator program
- ❑ **Test Item Listing, CRF** Use the Test Item Listing to identify questions to use in a customized homework, quiz, or test.

Parent Letter

Tobacco and Alcohol

Dear Parent/Guardian,

In the years to come, your son or daughter will be making decisions that impact his or her physical, emotional, and social health. The purpose of this Health Education class is to provide students with the knowledge and resources they need to make responsible and well-informed decisions about their health. As the course progresses, students will be asked to explore their values, opinions, and beliefs about health. It is important that students receive mature guidance in the classroom and at home as they address these issues.

In the next few weeks, your son or daughter's Health Education class will focus on the subject of tobacco and alcohol. Your child's ability to make good decisions about tobacco and alcohol use will influence not only how long he or she lives, but also the quality of his or her life years from now. The chapter will introduce strategies for resisting pressure to use alcohol and tobacco.

Other areas covered in this chapter include the short-term and long-term effects of tobacco and alcohol abuse. The class will also discuss addiction and the risks of driving while intoxicated.

You can actively support your child's progress in Health by communicating with him or her about the topics covered in this course. To aid in this communication, I have included a worksheet for you to complete with your child. This worksheet is an At-Home Activity entitled *Tobacco and Alcohol,* which provides guidance for more discussion. Your signature at the end of this material will verify that this home interaction has taken place.

Thank you in advance for your time, cooperation, and support.

Sincerely,

____

Health Teacher

Carta a los Padres/al Tutor

El tabaco y el alcohol

Estimado(s) Padres/Tutor:

En el futuro, su hijo/a va a hacer decisiones que influyan en su salud física, emocional y social. El propósito fundamental de la clase de Salud es proporcionarles a los estudiantes los conocimientos y recursos precisos para hacer responsables decisiones bien informadas en cuanto a su salud. Durante el año académico, los alumnos tendrán que revisar sus valores, opiniones y creencias sobre la salud. Es importante que, al confrontar estos asuntos, los jóvenes reciban informes y consejos de adultos tanto en el aula de clases como en casa.

En las próximas semanas, la clase de Salud se enfocará en el tema del tabaco y del alcohol. La capacidad de su hijo/a de hacer buenas decisiones sobre el uso del tabaco y del alcohol influirá tanto en cuántos años viva como en la calidad de aquellos años. El capítulo presentará estrategias para resistir la intimidación de usar el alcohol y el tabaco.

Otros asuntos tratados son los efectos de largo y corto plazo del abuso del tabaco y del alcohol. También se discutirán la adicción y los riesgos de manejar bajo la influencia del alcohol.

Ud. puede ayudar a su hijo/a en esta clase por hablar con él o ella sobre los temas que estudie. Para facilitar esta comunicación le mando una hoja de trabajo para una Actividad En Casa llamada El tabaco y el alcohol para completar con su hijo/a. Su firma en la hoja verifica que Uds. discutieron esta actividad juntos.

Gracias anticipadas por su tiempo, cooperación y apoyo.

Atentamente,

____

Maestro/a de Salud

Assesssment

Performance-Based Assessment

Refusing Tobacco and Alcohol

Teacher's Notes

INTRODUCTION

Students will choose a partner and write skits about refusing tobacco and alcohol. One student will write a skit in which a person is offered alcohol or tobacco and does not refuse. The skit will explore the consequences of not refusing the drug. The other student will write a different skit in which a person is offered alcohol or tobacco and does refuse. That skit will demonstrate what technique the person uses to refuse.

TIME REQUIRED One 45-minute class period

Students will need 15 minutes to write and practice their skits, and 30 minutes to perform their skits for the class and answer the analysis questions.

PBA RATINGS

Teacher Prep—1
Student Set-Up—3
Concept Level—2
Clean Up—1

ADVANCE PREPARATION

This activity works best with pairs of students. Decide if you will pair students or let them choose a partner.

PERFORMANCE

At the end of the test, students should turn in the following items:

- Written skit
- Worked with answers to analysis questions

EVALUATION

The following is a recommended breakdown for evaluating student performance:

30% Quality of written skit
30% Understanding of refusal skills
20% Performance of skit
20% Answers to analysis questions

Answer Key

Directed Reading

LESSON: TOBACCO AND ALCOHOL AS DRUGS

1. They are considered drugs because they affect the mind and body.
2. tobacco
3. Alcohol causes body functions to slow down.
4. body weight; how much food is in the stomach; how much they have used alcohol in the past

LESSON: TOBACCO PRODUCTS

5. b
6. Tar is a black, sticky substance that coats the lungs.
7. Answers may vary. Sample answer: bad breath, wrinkled skin, and difficulty breathing
8. ETS is a mixture of exhaled smoke and smoke from the ends of lit cigarettes.
9. coughing, shortness of breath, increased symptoms of allergies and asthma
10. d
11. Emphysema occurs when the lungs are so damaged that they cannot absorb enough oxygen. Cancer occurs when a group of cells grows uncontrollably and destroys healthy body tissue.

LESSON: ALCOHOL

12. Answers may vary. Sample answers: dizziness, vomiting, passing out
13. Intoxication is the state of being affected by alcohol.
14. blood alcohol concentration
15. c
16. d
17. fetal alcohol syndrome (FAS)
18. d

LESSON: ADDICITION

19. tolerance
20. drug addiction
21. Alcoholism is a disease caused by addiction to alcohol.
22. The body can become so dependent on alcohol that it physically needs the drug to function.
23. peer pressure
24. They depict drug use as glamorous or cool.
25. No, although drugs are often seen as an escape from problems, they may actually make problems worse.

LESSON: REFUSING TOBACCO AND ALCOHOL

26. Answers may vary. Sample answers: say "no, thanks," give a reason for refusing
27. Answers may vary. Sample answers: getting ice cream, going for a bike ride
28. Sample answer: No. Drugs can make it harder to be social when they cause confusion and tiredness.

Concept Mapping

LESSON: TOBACCO PRODUCTS

Tobacco products such as *cigarettes* produce *tar* and *carbon monoxide* which can cause *cancer* and *emphysema*; they also contain *nicotine*, which is an *addictive drug*.

LESSON: REFUSING TOBACCO AND ALCOHOL

Pressure to use tobacco and alcohol can come from *friends*, *advertisements*, and *role models*, and can be resisted with *refusal skills* such as *saying "no, thanks," giving a reason, suggesting an alternative*, or *walking away*.

Concept Review

LESSON: TOBACCO AND ALCOHOL AS DRUGS

1. d
2. They are drugs because they affect the mind and body.
3. They can affect different people differently, and their effects can change if they are mixed with another drug.

LESSON: TOBACCO PRODUCTS

4. It keeps the body from getting enough oxygen.
5. Tar coats the lungs and blocks oxygen from being absorbed. Tar can also keep the body from filtering out harmful particles in the air.
6. hair and clothes smell bad; bad breath; dulled taste buds
7. b
8. e
9. a
10. f
11. d
12. c

LESSON: ALCOHOL

13. Answers may vary. Sample answers: loss of control, lightheadedness, vomiting
14. blood alcohol concentration
15. Sample answer: cirrhosis, stomach ulcers
16. Alcohol slows a person's reaction time making it dangerous to drive.
17. Answers may vary. Sample answers: low birth weight, mental disabilities

LESSON: ADDICTION

18. c
19. a
20. b
21. Answers may vary. Sample answer: Alcoholism can be painful for family members. For example, children may not understand the behavior of their parents when they are drinking alcohol.
22. Alcoholics Anonymous, Al-Anon, Alateen
23. People may be unable to quit even though they want to. It can be dangerous to quit if the body is so dependent on alcohol that it physically needs the drug to function.

LESSON: FEELING PRESSURE

24. Friends may offer you a cigarette or a beer. Family members may use tobacco or alcohol in front of you, making it seem OK. Role models may make drug use seem safe.
25. It can be negative because peers may pressure you to try tobacco or alcohol. It can be positive because other peers may pressure you to avoid these drugs.
26. The media may make tobacco and alcohol look glamorous or cool.

LESSON: REFUSING TOBACCO AND ALCOHOL

27. Answers may vary. Sample answers: Say "no, thanks." Give a reason for refusing, such as "it's illegal."
28. Answers may vary. Sample answers: join a music group, a theater group, or a volunteer program

Refusal Skills

LESSON: FEELING PRESSURE

Answers may vary. Sample answers:

1. I am not interested in smoking.
2. I could offer her a stick of gum.
3. I would tell her that smoking is unhealthy, and I do not want to suffer the consequences of smoking.
4. Sorry, but I think I will walk the rest of the way by myself.
5. I could stop walking home with Joanna. I could ask my sister to practice with me.
6. I have friends who do not smoke. They will stand by my decision not to smoke.

LESSON: REFUSING TOBACCO AND ALCOHOL

Letters may vary. Sample letter:

Dear Trying,

Next time, try saying "No, thank you." You could also offer a reason for refusing, such as it is illegal to drink alcohol at your age. It is important to remember that your true friends will respect your decision to avoid alcohol. If these people still pressure you, you can always just leave the party.

Sincerely,

Know-It-All

Decision-Making Skills

LESSON: TOBACCO PRODUCTS

Answers may vary. Accept all reasonable answers. Sample answers:

1. I must decide if I will smoke or not.
2. My health is important to me.

3. I could start smoking, continue to go to the park and not smoke, or stop going to the park with my friends.
4. If I start smoking, my health will suffer. If I continue to go to the park but don't smoke, my health will still suffer from secondhand smoke. If I stop going to the park, I won't get to hang out with Bill and Dennis as much, but I will protect my health.
5. I will stop going to the park. This way I know I'll keep myself healthy.
6. I am happy with my decision. It was a good one, and I'd do it again. Although I do not see Bill and Dennis as much anymore, I met some new friends who do not smoke.

LESSON: ALCOHOL

Story endings may vary. Sample ending: Even though Walter knew his parents would be angry with him, he knew it was too risky to get in the car with Carrie. He decided to call his parents. They were very upset with him for lying to them and grounded him for a month. But they told Walter they were glad he had called for a ride. Also, Walter was happy with his decision because he got a safe ride home. He decided not to go to any more parties where he knew alcohol would be served.

Cross-Disciplinary: Music

LESSON: TOBACCO AND ALCOHOL AS DRUGS

Students' jingles may vary. Ask them to perform their song for the class.

Cross-Disciplinary: Language Arts

LESSON: ALCOHOL

Students' plays may vary, but should show one character who is intoxicated. If students perform their plays, be careful that the intoxicated student doesn't get too rough or out of control.

Quiz

LESSON: TOBACCO AND ALCOHOL AS DRUGS

1. d
2. b
3. d
4. d
5. a

LESSON: TOBACCO PRODUCTS

1. d
2. a
3. b
4. c
5. d
6. d

LESSON: ALCOHOL

1. d
2. c
3. a
4. b
5. a
6. d

LESSON: ADDICTION

1. b
2. a
3. d
4. c
5. a

LESSON: FEELING PRESSURE

1. d
2. b
3. d
4. a
5. c

LESSON: REFUSING TOBACCO AND ALCOHOL

1. d
2. c
3. d
4. d
5. b

Chapter Test

TOBACCO AND ALCOHOL

1. intoxication
2. alcohol
3. alcoholism
4. cancer

5. peer pressure
6. blood alcohol concentration
7. c
8. b
9. b
10. d
11. a
12. b
13. d
14. a
15. People react differently to a drug based on their body weight, how much food is in the stomach, and how much they have used the drug in the past.
16. Carbon monoxide is absorbed by the lungs and keeps the body from getting enough oxygen. Tar coats the lungs and can block oxygen from being absorbed. It can also keep the body from filtering out harmful particles in the air.
17. BAC is affected by the amount of alcohol a person drinks and by his or her body weight.
18. Advertisements make tobacco and alcohol use look glamorous or cool. Some people think that if they use alcohol or tobacco, they will look like the people in the advertisements.
19. Tolerance is the body's ability to resist the effects of a drug. It causes a person to need more of a drug in order to feel its original effects. When tolerance gets stronger, the body can start to feel uncomfortable without the drug. When a person needs the drug to feel normal, the condition is called drug addiction.
20. Answers may vary. Sample answer: Serena could say "no, thanks." She could say she doesn't want to drink it because it's illegal. She could also suggest an alternative activity such as watching a video.
21. About 70 percent want to quit.
22. About 3 percent are successful in quitting smoking.
23. Answers may vary. Sample answer: It encourages me not to start smoking because it is very unlikely that I would be able to quit.

Performance-Based Assessment

6. Answers may vary. Sample answer: Underage alcohol use is illegal and it can get you into a lot of trouble with the police and with your parents. It can also lead to being stuck in a dangerous situation.
7. Answers may vary. Sample answer: The person could have said, "no thanks" and walked away.
8. Answers may vary. Sample answer: The person said, "no thanks" and pointed out that underage smoking is illegal.
9. Answers may vary. Accept all reasonable responses.

Datasheet for In-Text Activity

1. The smallest glass that received three drops of blue food coloring would have the highest BAC. The glass that received one drop of blue food coloring will have the lowest BAC (unless one of the other glasses is big enough that the color after three drops of blue food coloring is lighter than the glass that received one drop).
2. A larger glass will have a lower BAC when receiving the same amount of "alcohol." A smaller glass will have a higher BAC when receiving the same amount of "alcohol."

Life Skills: Communicating Effectively

LESSON: ADDICTION

1. Yes, Nora is probably suffering from alcoholism. She is drinking a lot both at home and at school.
2. Answers may vary. Sample answer: I could tell Nora that I am worried about her and offer to get her some help.
3. Answers may vary. Sample answer: I could suggest that Nora talk to her parents and tell them that she needs help.

4. Answers may vary. Sample answer: I will talk to my parents or a teacher about my concerns.

Life Skills: Evaluating Media Messages

LESSON: FEELING PRESSURE

1. Students' magazine choices may vary.
2. Students' responses may vary based on magazine choices.
3. Students' responses may vary based on the ads they examined.
4. Students' responses may vary based on the ads they examined.
5. Answers may vary. Sample answer: These ads make tobacco and alcohol use look glamorous, but they do not show the dangers involved.

Enrichment Activities

LESSON: TOBACCO AND ALCOHOL AS DRUGS

Students should create one graph showing the percentage of students who think tobacco is a drug compared with the percentage of those who do not. The other graph should show the percentage of students who think alcohol is a drug compared with the percentage of those who do not. Students should write a paragraph explaining whether or not they were surprised by the results of their survey.

LESSON: TOBACCO PRODUCTS

Students should write three paragraphs that summarize their interview with an adult who is a long-time smoker.

LESSON: ALCOHOL

Students should write a one-page report that summarizes their research on the laws regarding driving while intoxicated in their state.

LESSON: ADDICTION

Students should prepare an oral presentation that summarizes their findings on alcoholism. Reports should include the number of people in the United States who suffer from alcoholism, a description of support programs, and rehabilitation programs.

LESSON: FEELING PRESSURE

Students' collages should include ads that glamorize the use of alcohol and tobacco. They should paste the negative effects of alcohol and tobacco use over the glamorous images. Hang the collages in the classroom.

LESSON: REFUSING TOBACCO AND ALCOHOL

Students' scripts should include a discussion of different ways to say no; how to provide alternatives; and a list of social activities that do not involve alcohol and tobacco products.

Health Inventory

Students' responses may vary. This worksheet can be used to start a discussion on peer pressure to use alcohol and tobacco products.

Health Behavior Contract

Accept all reasonable responses.

At-Home Activity

1. Student responses may vary based on the advertisement they chose.
2. Student responses may vary based on the advertisement they chose.
3. Student responses may vary based on the advertisement they chose.
4. Student responses may vary based on the advertisement they chose.

TEST ITEM LISTING

Tobacco and Alcohol

MULTIPLE CHOICE

1. Tobacco
   a. is a drug.
   b. can make people feel more alert.
   c. can make people feel more relaxed.
   d. All of the above

   Answer: D Difficulty: 1 Section: 1 Objective: 1

2. Which is NOT an effect of alcohol?
   a. It lowers heart rate.
   b. It speeds reaction time.
   c. It lowers breathing rate.
   d. It slows the mind.

   Answer: B Difficulty: 1 Section: 1 Objective: 1

3. Tobacco is used to make products such as
   a. cigars.
   b. smokeless tobacco.
   c. cigarettes.
   d. All of the above

   Answer: D Difficulty: 1 Section: 1 Objective: 1

4. Which factor affects how a person reacts to a drug?
   a. how much food is in their stomach
   b. their body weight
   c. how much they have used the drug in the past
   d. All of the above

   Answer: D Difficulty: 1 Section: 1 Objective: 1

5. Mixing alcohol or tobacco with another drug can
   a. change its effects.
   b. be good for you.
   c. help you solve your problems.
   d. None of the above

   Answer: A Difficulty: 1 Section: 1 Objective: 1

6. One dangerous chemical found in all tobacco products is
   a. carbon monoxide.
   b. tar.
   c. ETS.
   d. nicotine.

   Answer: D Difficulty: 1 Section: 2 Objective: 1

7. A dangerous gas in cigarette smoke is
   a. carbon monoxide.
   b. tar.
   c. ETS.
   d. nicotine.

   Answer: A Difficulty: 1 Section: 2 Objective: 1

8. A sticky substance that coats the lungs is
   a. carbon monoxide.
   b. tar.
   c. ETS.
   d. nicotine.
   Answer: B Difficulty: 1 Section: 2 Objective: 1
9. The mixture of exhaled smoke and smoke from the end of a cigarette is called
   a. carbon monoxide.
   b. tar.
   c. ETS.
   d. nicotine.
   Answer: C Difficulty: 1 Section: 2 Objective: 1
10. Some effects of cigarettes include
   a. dulled taste buds.
   b. yellow teeth.
   c. difficulty breathing.
   d. All of the above
   Answer: D Difficulty: 1 Section: 2 Objective: 2
11. Which is a harmless form of tobacco?
   a. snuff
   b. chewing tobacco
   c. spit tobacco
   d. None of the above
   Answer: D Difficulty: 1 Section: 2 Objective: 2
12. How does alcohol affect a person's ability to drive?
   a. It slows your reaction time.
   b. It makes you see more clearly.
   c. It makes you more alert.
   d. All of the above
   Answer: A Difficulty: 1 Section: 3 Objective: 3
13. Which is an effect of intoxication?
   a. vomiting
   b. passing out
   c. tiredness
   d. All of the above
   Answer: D Difficulty: 1 Section: 3 Objective: 1
14. The body's ability to resist the effects of a drug is called
   a. drug addiction.
   b. tolerance.
   c. alcoholism.
   d. None of the above
   Answer: B Difficulty: 1 Section: 4 Objective: 1
15. Needing a drug to feel normal is called
   a. drug addiction.
   b. tolerance.
   c. alcoholism.
   d. None of the above
   Answer: A Difficulty: 1 Section: 4 Objective: 1

16. Which is an effect of alcoholism?
    a. difficulty making decisions
    b. strange reactions to normal events
    c. neglecting family and friends
    d. All of the above

    Answer: D Difficulty: 2 Section: 4 Objective: 1

17. What can help people who have alcoholism and their families?
    a. smoking
    b. more alcohol
    c. support programs
    d. None of the above

    Answer: C Difficulty: 1 Section: 4 Objective: 2

18. Quitting an addiction to alcohol may require
    a. hospitalization.
    b. the person to give up.
    c. small bits of alcohol to help the person get by.
    d. All of the above

    Answer: A Difficulty: 1 Section: 4 Objective: 2

19. Pressure to try tobacco or alcohol can come from
    a. family members.
    b. friends.
    c. role models.
    d.All of the above

    Answer: D Difficulty: 1 Section: 5 Objective: 1

20. Influence from a friend or group of friends is called
    a. addiction.
    b. peer pressure.
    c. quitting.
    d. None of the above

    Answer: B Difficulty: 1 Section: 5 Objective: 1

21. How can advertisements encourage people to use tobacco and drugs?
    a. They make it look cool.
    b. They do not show the negative side of drug use.
    c. They make it look glamorous.
    d. All of the above

    Answer: D Difficulty: 1 Section: 5 Objective: 3

22. Abusing tobacco and drugs will NOT
    a. solve your problems.
    b. cause you to become addicted.
    c. negatively affect your health.
    d. All of the above

    Answer: A Difficulty: 1 Section: 5 Objective: 1

23. You can solve problems by
    a. drinking alcohol.
    b. smoking cigarettes.
    c. talking with others.
    d. None of the above

    Answer: C Difficulty: 1 Section: 5 Objective: 1

24. If If you are not comfortble giving reasons for refusing drugs, you could just
    a. change the subject.
    b. walk away.
    c. offer an alternative
    d. All of the above

    Answer: D Difficulty: 1 Section: 6 Objective: 1

25. A true friend will
    a. pressure you into using drugs.
    b. make fun of you if you refuse drugs.
    c. respect your decision to refuse drugs.
    d. All of the above

    Answer: C Difficulty: 1 Section: 6 Objective: 1

26. Which of the following is NOT a good excuse for refusing to do drugs?
    a. It's illegal.
    b. No thanks, I'm not interested.
    c. No thanks, I want to be ready for the game tomorrow.
    d. Maybe I'll try it later, after school.

    Answer: D Difficulty: 1 Section: 6 Objective: 1

27. Which is an example of a drug-free social activity?
    a. sports team
    b. volunteer program
    c. music group
    d. All of the above

    Answer: D Difficulty: 1 Section: 6 Objective: 2

28. Illegal drugs are
    a. the only way to have fun.
    b. dangerous and unpredictable.
    c. good for you.
    d. All of the above

    Answer: B Difficulty: 1 Section: 6 Objective: 2

29. A disease in which the liver is damaged and does not work normally is called
    a. cancer.
    b. FAS.
    c. cirrhosis.
    d. emphysema.

    Answer: C Difficulty: 1 Section: 3 Objective: 2

30. Another name for ETS is
    a. tobacco.
    b. secondhand smoke.
    c. nicotine.
    d. tar.

    Answer: B Difficulty: 1 Section: 2 Objective: 1

31. A disease that affects the unborn babies of women who drink alcohol during pregnancy is called
    a. cancer.
    b. FAS.
    c. cirrhosis.
    d. emphysema.

    Answer: B Difficulty: 1 Section: 3 Objective: 2

32. A disease in which the lungs get so damaged that they cannot absorb enough oxygen is called
    a. cancer.
    b. FAS.
    c. cirrhosis.
    d. emphysema.

    Answer: D Difficulty: 1 Section: 2 Objective: 2

33. A plant with leaves that can be dried and mixed with chemicals to make cigarettes and other products is called
    a. tobacco.
    b. nicotine.
    c. alcohol.
    d. tar.

    Answer: A Difficulty: 1 Section: 1 Objective: 1

34. The addictive drug found in cigarettes is
    a. nicotine.
    b. carbon monoxide.
    c. tar.
    d. ETS.

    Answer: A Difficulty: 1 Section: 2 Objective: 1

35. The percentage of alcohol in a person's blood is called
    a. blood intoxication.
    b. cirrhosis.
    c. intoxication.
    d. blood alcohol concentration.

    Answer: D Difficulty: 1 Section: 3 Objective: 1

36. Which is NOT an early effect of cigarette smoking?
    a. emphysema
    b. bad breath
    c. smelly clothes and hair
    d. dulled taste buds

    Answer: A Difficulty: 1 Section: 2 Objective: 1

37. Which is a symptom of breathing in environmental tobacco smoke?
    a. coughing
    b. shortness of breath
    c. feeling sick
    d. All of the above

    Answer: D Difficulty: 1 Section: 2 Objective: 1

38. Which is an effect of smokeless tobacco?
    a. bad breath
    b. tooth decay
    c. cuts and sores in the mouth
    d. All of the above

    Answer: D Difficulty: 1 Section: 2 Objective: 2

39. Tobacco use can eventually lead to
    a. cancer.
    b. death.
    c. emphysema.
    d. All of the above

    Answer: D Difficulty: 1 Section: 2 Objective: 3

40. Quitting an addiction can be
    a. easy.
    b. fun.
    c. dangerous.
    d. None of the above

    Answer: C Difficulty: 1 Section: 4 Objective: 2

41. People sometimes turn to drugs to
    a. escape problems.
    b. relieve stress.
    c. solve problems.
    d. All of the above

    Answer: D Difficulty: 1 Section: 5 Objective: 1

42. Which is NOT a good way to refuse tobacco or alcohol.
    a. Try it just once.
    b. Give a reason for refusing.
    c. Say "no, thanks."
    d. Offer an alternative.

    Answer: A Difficulty: 1 Section: 5 Objective: 2

COMPLETION

43. The state of being affected by alcohol is called ____________________.
    Answer: intoxication Difficulty: 1 Section: 3 Objective: 1
44. A liquid that can affect the way people think and act is ____________________.
    Answer: alcohol Difficulty: 1 Section: 1 Objective: 1
45. The disease caused by addiction to alcohol is called ____________________.
    Answer: alcoholism Difficulty: 1 Section: 4 Objective: 1
46. A long-term effect of using tobacco products is ____________________.
    Answer: cancer Difficulty: 2 Section: 2 Objective: 3
47. Encouragement from a friend to smoke a cigarette or drink alcohol is called ____________________.
    Answer: peer pressure
    Difficulty: 1 Section: 5 Objective: 1
48. The percentage of alcohol in a person's blood is called the ____________________.
    Answer: blood alcohol concentration
    Difficulty: 1 Section: 3 Objective: 1
49. A plant with leaves that can be dried and mixed with chemicals is ____________________.
    Answer: tobacco Difficulty: 1 Section: 1 Objective: 1
50. Powdered tobacco that can be sniffed into the nose is called ____________________.
    Answer: snuff Difficulty: 1 Section: 2 Objective: 2
51. A disease caused by tobacco in which the lungs get so damaged that they cannot absorb enough oxygen is called ____________________.
    Answer: emphysema
    Difficulty: 1 Section: 2 Objective: 3
52. Unborn babies can suffer from ____________________ if their mother's drink alcohol during pregnancy.
    Answer: fetal alcohol syndrome (FAS)
    Difficulty: 1 Section: 3 Objective: 2
53. A person's ability to resist the effects of a drug is called ____________________.
    Answer: tolerance Difficulty: 1 Section: 2 Objective: 2
54. Needing a drug to feel normal is called ____________________.
    Answer: drug addiction
    Difficulty: 1 Section: 4 Objective: 2
55. A disease that damages the liver of people who consume large quantities of alcohol is ____________________.
    Answer: cirrhosis Difficulty: 1 Section: 3 Objective: 2

SHORT ANSWER

56. Explain the factors that affect how people will react to a drug.
    Answer:
    People react differently to a drug based on their body weight, how much food is in the stomach, and how much they have used the drug in the past.
    Difficulty: 2 Section: 1 Objective: 2

57. Explain how carbon monoxide and tar damage the body.
    Answer:
    Carbon monoxide is absorbed by the lungs and keeps the body from getting enough oxygen. Tar coats the lungs and can block oxygen from being absorbed. It can also keep the body from filtering out harmful particles in the air.
    Difficulty: 2 Section: 2 Objective: 1

58. Explain what affects blood alcohol concentration.
    Answer:
    BAC is affected by the amount of alcohol a person drinks and by body weight.
    Difficulty: 1 Section: 3 Objective: 1

59. Explain how advertisements can be a source of pressure to use tobacco and alcohol.
    Answer:
    Advertisements make people look glamorous or cool. Some people think that if they use alcohol or tobacco, they will look like the people in the advertisement.
    Difficulty: 2 Section: 5 Objective: 3

60. Name three factors that affect how a person reacts to alcohol.
    Answer:
    body weight, amount of food in the stomach, how much the person has used alcohol in the past
    Difficulty: 1 Section: 1 Objective: 1

61. Why is it dangerous to mix alcohol with other drugs?
    Answer:
    Mixing drugs with alcohol may change the effects of the alcohol or the other drugs.
    Difficulty: 1 Section: 1 Objective: 1

62. Name and describe two chemicals found in tobacco products.
    Sample answer:
    Nicotine is an addictive drug that causes people to want more cigarettes. Carbon monoxide is a dangerous gas that keeps the body from getting enough oxygen.
    Difficulty: 2 Section: 2 Objective: 1

63. Describe the harmful effects of inhaling environmental tobacco smoke.
    Answer:
    coughing, shortness of breath, allergies, asthma, and tar and chemicals building up in the lungs
    Difficulty: 1 Section: 2 Objective: 1

64. What tobacco product can cause the inside of the nose to decay?
    Answer: snuff
    Difficulty: 1 Section: 2 Objective: 2

65. What are some effects of FAS?
    Sample answer:
    Low birth weight, mental impairments, physical deformities, and behavioral problems
    Difficulty: 2 Section: 3 Objective: 2

66. Which has more alcohol—a beer or a glass of wine?
    Answer: A beer has the same amount of alcohol as a glass of wine.
    Difficulty: 1 Section: 3 Objective: 1

67. What is tolerance?
    Answer: Tolerance is the body's ability to resist the effects of a drug.
    Difficulty: 1 Section: 4 Objective: 1

68. Can people become addicted to a drug without realizing it is happening?
    Answer: yes
    Difficulty: 1 Section: 4 Objective: 1

69. List three support groups for alcoholics and their families.
    Answer: Alcoholics Anonymous, Al-Anon, and Alateen
    Difficulty: 1 Section: 4 Objective: 2

70. Describe three examples of negative peer pressure.
    Sample answer:
    a friend offers me a cigarette, friends smoking or drinking around me, watching family members smoke
    Difficulty: 2 Section: 5 Objective: 2

71. What are some negative effects of using tobacco that advertisements do not show?
    Sample answer:
    Tobacco can make it harder to breathe, cause skin to wrinkle, cause teeth to turn yellow, and lead to cancer or other serious diseases.
    Difficulty: 2 Section: 5 Objective: 3

72. What could you do to make new friends?
    Answer: join a group with people who share a common interest
    Difficulty: 1 Section: 6 Objective: 2

73. What questions should you ask yourself when a friend pressures you to try a drug after you have made it clear that you do not want to try drugs?
    Sample answer:
    Why would another person want me to take drugs? Is this person being a good friend?
    Difficulty: 2 Section: 6 Objective: 1

74. What can you do if you are uncomfortable giving a reason for refusing drugs?
    Sample answer:
    change the subject by suggesting something fun to do instead of doing drugs.
    Difficulty: 2 Section: 6 Objective: 1

75. Explain why tobacco and alcohol are considered drugs.
    Answer: They affect the mind and body.
    Difficulty: 1 Section: 1 Objective: 1

76. List two types of smokeless tobacco.
    Answer: snuff, chewing tobacco
    Difficulty: 1 Section: 2 Objective: 2

77. List two diseases caused by long-term tobacco use.
    Sample answer: emphysema, cancer
    Difficulty: 1 Section: 2 Objective: 3

78. Define blood alcohol concentration (BAC)
    Answer: the percentage of alcohol in a person's blood
    Difficulty: 1 Section: 2 Objective: 1

MATCHING

a. intoxication
b. blood alcohol concentration
c. cirrhosis
d. fetal alcohol syndrome
e. tobacco
f. alcohol
g. ETS
h. nicotine

79. ____ a disease prevents the liver from working normally
Answer: C Difficulty: 1 Section: 3 Objective: 2
80. ____ a group of birth defects that can occur when an unborn baby is exposed to alcohol
Answer: D Difficulty: 1 Section: 3 Objective: 1
81. ____ percentage of alcohol in the blood
Answer: B Difficulty: 1 Section: 3 Objective: 1
82. ____ state of being affected by alcohol
Answer: A Difficulty: 1 Section: 3 Objective: 1
83. ____ liquid that can affect the way people think and act
Answer: F Difficulty: 1 Section: 1 Objective: 1
84. ____ a mixture of inhaled smoke and smoke from the ends of a lit cigarette
Answer: G Difficulty: 1 Section: 2 Objective: 1
85. ____ plant with leaves that can be dried and mixed with other chemicals
Answer: E Difficulty: 1 Section: 1 Objective: 1
86. ____ an addictive drug found in all tobacco products
Answer: H Difficulty: 1 Section: 2 Objective: 1

ESSAY

87. Explain how tolerance is related to drug addiction.
Answer:
Tolerance is the ability to resist the effects of a drug. It causes the person to need more of the drug in order to feel its original effects. When tolerance gets stronger, the body can start to feel uncomfortable without the drug. When a person needs a drug to feel normal, the condition is called drug addiction.
Difficulty: 2 Section: 4 Objective: 2

80. Serena is spending the night at her friend Emily's house. After Emily's parents go to bed, Emily opens up the refrigerator and pours a glass of wine for herself and Serena. Describe and explain three ways that Serena could refuse the alcohol.
Sample answer:
Serena could say "no, thanks." She could say she doesn't want to drink it because it's illegal. She could also suggest an alternative activity such as watching a video.
Difficulty: 2 Section: 6 Objective: 1

INTERPRETING GRAPHICS

Examine the diagram below, and answer the question that follows.

89. About what percentage of smokers want to quit?
    Answer: About 70 percent want to quit.
    Difficulty: 2 Section: 4 Objective: 2

90. About what percentage of succeed in permanently quitting?
    Answer: About 3 percent are successful in quitting smoking.
    Difficulty: 2 Section: 4 Objective: 2

91. How does looking at this graph influence your decision to start smoking or not?
    Sample answer:
    It encourages me not to start smoking because it is very unlikely that I would be able to quit.
    Difficulty: 1 Section: 4 Objective: 2

9997256522 1 2 3 4 5 6